EDITOR: MARTIN WINDROW

OSPREY MILITARY

MEN-AT-ARMS SERIES 231

FRENCH MEDIEVAL ARMIES 1000-1300

Text by
DAVID NICOLLE, PhD
Colour plates by
ANGUS McBRIDE

D0880339

First published in Great Britain in 1991 by
Osprey, a division of Reed Consumer Books Limited,
Michelin House, 81 Fulham Road,
London SW3 6RB
and Auckland, Melbourne, Singapore and Toronto

Reprinted 1993, 1994, 1997

British Library Cataloguing in Publication Data
Nicolle, David *1944–*
   French medieval armies.
   1. France. Armee. history
   I. Title
   355.00944

ISBN 1-85532-127-0

Filmset in Great Britain
Printed through World Print Ltd, Hong Kong

Dedication
For Brendan and Emily
bons fruits des Gaéls et des Gauls

Artist's Note
Readers may care to note that the original paintings
from which the colour plates in this book were
prepared are available for private sale. All
reproduction copyright whatsoever is retained by the
publisher. All enquiries should be addressed to:
   Scorpio
   PO Box 475,
   Hailsham,
   E. Sussex BN27 2SL
The publishers regret that they can enter into no
correspondence upon this matter.

better off, and by 1100 many had become major hereditary landowners. Even in military terms the first *miles* was not necessarily a cavalryman, and in the early 12th century there were still references to a few *milites pedites* (infantry 'knights'); yet there was already more to being a *miles*, who should normally own armour, helmet, shield, sword and lance.

For a while in the late 11th and early 12th centuries the Church's efforts to tame the *milites* almost turned them into a quasi-religious class of 'holy warriors', but this failed, and a drive for domination took over from ideals of service. By the 12th century the great nobles of France had abandoned cities for castles; and while the Church now glorified the *miles*, the *miles*' role in turn gradually ennobled him in a world fragmented into small lordships grouped around local castles. The *milites* did not become a fixed warrior caste until the late 12th century; but once they did, their sense of exclusiveness made it difficult for kings or great lords to raise new knights. The nobility was already divided according to rank, though this was not clear cut. At the top were the *bannerets*, then the fief-holding knights, the enlisted knights or *chevaliers engagé*, and lastly the squires.

Training

The military élite were all trained in much the same way, their education starting at the age of five. This was described, idealistically perhaps, as 'rising early from a bed of fox-skins beneath a statue of St. Christopher'. The boy served his father, learned chess and riding and had religious instruction. At the age of seven he should be taken away from the women to become a page, when he would continue to ride, hunt and learn to use a sword, lance and other weapons. Stag hunting and falconry could be dangerous but also gave the boy his first lessons in fieldcraft and tactics. At 12 he might be sent to complete his education in the household of a noted lord, where life could be tough. Two years later he might start looking after the dogs and at 20 he could be a fully trained huntsman. Meanwhile the youth learned good manners, cleanliness, singing and music.

To become a squire the young man attended a church ceremony when a priest gave him a sword, belt and scabbard. The new squire was also encouraged to fight, travel, and learn about the world.

'David and Goliath', Bible of St. Etienne, 1109–11. The helmet and long kite-shaped shield used by Goliath are the same as those in the famous Anglo-Norman Bayeux Tapestry. Only the long sleeves of the mail hauberk distinguish this as late 11th century equipment. (Ms. 168, f.5r, Bib. Munic., Dijon)

To be dubbed a knight was a more solemn occasion. In its fully developed 13th-century form dubbing involved the *poursuivant* squire, dressed in a plain white shirt and drawers, enduring a lonely vigil in church before the service.

Although a few knights learned to read in the 12th century, the *jeunes*' or young warrior's training remained military, and was carried out within a small band of *amis* or companions who formed a *compagnie* or *maisnie*. Handling weapons and manoeuvring together in a closely packed unit of lance-armed cavalry were basic skills. Teamwork was paramount, training dangerous, and the knight's subsequent career even more hazardous: in one recorded group of 15 *amis* three died in battle and one in a fall from a horse. Great emphasis was laid on keeping weapons in good condition through constant cleaning and oiling, the *Chansons de Geste* pouring scorn on those unable to draw rusty blades from their scabbards. In the 12th century, despite a fashion for flowing locks, the *Chansons* also advised a warrior to shave and cut his hair before battle, not only to make his helmet fit properly but to show proper respect for his foe.

'Life of St. Nicholas', carved font from northern France, 1150–75. The axe was a common 12th century infantry weapon. (Winchester Cathedral; author's photograph)

equipment remained basically the same until the later 13th century.

Even as early as the mid-12th century, however, complete arms had become too expensive for non-noble warriors, professional *sergeants* being equipped by the nobles who maintained them. There was also plenty of variation in the quality and quantity of weaponry and horses among the knights, which betrayed rank as well as wealth. Twelfth-century status ran from the humble *milites rustici*, *milites gregarii* and *milites plebei* to the leading *primi milites* or *strenui milites*. A century later such differences were enshrined in a rigid class system, from the squires and young *bachelers*, through the *chevalier d'un ecu*, to the leading *bannerets*. Each rank was expected to have a specified minimum of equipment, plus a certain number of horses and followers. Generally speaking a 13th-century knight should have two companions and three horses—a good *destrier* or war-horse and two ordinary riding horses—while a *banneret* should have at least five followers and two *destriers*. By this time warfare was not particularly dangerous for a fully armoured knight; and it was normally considered foolish to kill a man of one's own rank—this not only lost a ransom, but invited a blood feud with the victim's family. Even war-horses were too valuable to kill carelessly.

Feudal service

Forty days was the normal annual period of feudal service, and before an expansion of trade brought more money into circulation in the 12th century such military obligations gave great power to the early *milites*. As the importance of infantry and unarmoured cavalry declined, they remained the most effective warriors available to an ambitious nobleman. Each French lord, including a king who was still little more than first among equals, had to rely on troops from his own territory. The king had the Royal Domain centred upon Paris from which to summon his immediate vassal knights, plus infantry raised by the towns and officials in each *prévôté* or military region. Only if France was invaded by a foreign army could the king rely on direct help from his great nobles. Vassals could be summoned for various kinds of military service, such as the *chevauchée* to defend a lord's own territory, or the *ost* outside such territory. Thirdly there was the *estaige* or summons to garrison

Equipment and rank

The *miles*' equipment also became more expensive. A horse could cost five times as much as a bull, a war-horse rising from four times the value of an ordinary horse in the 8th century to seven times in the late 13th. A late 11th-century mail hauberk might be worth no less than ten bulls; and while not every *miles* owned his own horse and hauberk, booty remained vital to the rising knight. Those who lost their horses in battle would still be considered knights but were expected to re-equip themselves rapidly. Before the battle a fully equipped 12th-century *miles* would first put on his leg defences, then the padding worn beneath his mail hauberk. Next came the hauberk itself, his sword-belt and helmet. The knight would take his shield and lance after mounting his horse. Details of shape and weight changed, but such a lord's castle, the centre of his *châtellenie*. But as money flowed more freely so the power of military vassals over their lords declined, since the richer nobility could now enlist mercenaries.

Four kinds of knight also emerged: the nobles who were powerful enough to raise followers and fight in their own interests; the landed vassals who fought for their lords as a feudal obligation; *ministerial* knights, who lacked fiefs but lived at a lord's court as his retainers; and mercenary knights who fought for pay. A man could, of course, play more than one role during his life. By the 13th century many fief-holders no longer fought for their lord but paid taxes with which he hired mercenaries. The increasing wealth of the crown also made royal knights more like mercenaries, their losses being replaced by a paymaster who also encouraged them to serve for more than the normal 40 days. By the first years of the 13th century the French king could maintain a virtual standing army on his frontier with English-ruled Normandy. In 1202–3 this included 257 knights, 267 mounted sergeants, 80 mounted crossbowmen, 133 infantry crossbowmen, 2,000 other infantry and 300 specifically mercenary troops.

The growing importance of non-noble but professional *sergeants* reflected these changes. Many seem to have been recruited from families which could no longer afford the status of *milites*, though often retaining small fiefs. Their role remained basically the same as that of knights, with comparable equipment being supplied by their employers. During the 13th century the proportion of knights further declined in favour of squires, many of whom could similarly not afford to be dubbed knights. By the early 14th century squires outnumbered knights by no less than ten to one in some French armies.

The knights, whether feudal vassals or paid mercenaries, needed the support of squires, horse-breeders, armourers and others. The squire himself had mixed origins. Back in the 11th century a *miles* would generally be followed by a servant or *armiger* who looked after his equipment. Though mounted,

this *armiger* was not armoured. *Armigeri* were still recorded in the 13th century when they were well-paid, fully equipped warriors, though lower in rank than knights, and were often grouped with the squires. Another confusing 11th and 12th century term is *bacheler*. Some have seen him as a young warrior not yet knighted, or as an early squire; however, it seems that the word *bacheler* simply described the youthful enthusiasm of a young 'hero' and not his status.

Squires actually emerged in the early 12th century as non-noble warriors, fighting alongside *sergeants* in sieges, foraging for supplies and pillaging

'Guard playing a viol', Atlantic Bible, south French, late 11th century. The most interesting piece of armour is this man's round-topped one-piece helmet; these were seen in the Mediterranean lands, and probably reflected Byzantine or Islamic influence. (Ms. Edili 126–6, f.124v, Bib. Laurenziana, Florence)

the dead. The 12th century northern French squire was attached to a knight and would erect his tent, look after his horse, collect firewood and water; he would ride behind, carrying the knight's spear and shield and leading his *destrier*. In battle the squire would take his master's *palfrey* or riding horse and mule, then withdraw under the command of a *gonfanonier*. A rich knight might have a second squire who rode into battle behind him, leading a spare war-horse. Only in emergencies were squires given full equipment and sent into battle. By the 13th century the care of horses remained a squire's primary task, although he often possessed basic arms and was also expected to fight. Differences between various ranks of squire, such as *scutiferi*, *servientes*, *armigeri* and *valetti*, largely disappeared by the mid-13th century, while squires as a whole rose in prestige. The knights were now an élite minority, while lesser military duties such as collecting and guarding prisoners, protecting the baggage, carrying a knight's lance and forming a rearguard fell to the squires.

The knight's domination of the battlefield, though exaggerated, was secure until new weapons and tactics eventually unseated him. Even the failure of Western heavy cavalry in the Crusades and the development of crossbows took several centuries to undermine the knight's prestige. Yet the threat posed by horse-archery and the crossbow reinforced a prejudice against all forms of missile weapon in 12th and 13th century Western Europe. This extended to javelins, stones and siege artillery. Neglect of archery was not a quirk of the French feudal mentality but an effort to suppress weapons that challenged the existing military order. Such attitudes were enshrined in the *Chansons de Geste* which reflected and strengthened the knightly ideals. Saint Maurice had already been adopted as the patron saint of knights, and the Church also lent its weight to prejudices against anything except close combat. In 1139 the second Lateran Council attempted to ban the use not only of crossbows but even of ordinary hand bows in warfare—except against 'infidels'.

Knightly ideals

Meanwhile the qualities expected of knights by the Church and members of the knightly élite grew. In the late 11th century these included abstinence from looting and homicide (which posed some problems!) as well as chastity (which clashed with the rising cult of Courtly Love). Then there was 'courtesy' which meant being considerate and merciful to fellow knights, as well as striving for a warlike reputation, generosity (particularly to the minstrels who publicised a knight's reputation), loyalty, the skill at arms which marked a man of true *prowess*, obedience to the Church, and protection of the weak.

During the 11th century priests also became involved in dubbing ceremonies as part of the Church's effort to control the turbulent *milites*. Yet

'Horsemen of the Apocalypse', Beatus of St. Sever, *south-west French, 1028–72. The horses have saddles which are between the original Arab-Islamic* form and the fully developed 12th century European jousting saddle. (Ms. Lat. 8878, f.109r, Bib. Nat., Paris)

the moral problems faced by a knight were inherent in his role as a fighting man, in his duty to his lord and his loyalty to his fellows. This was clearly recognised by churchmen like the 12th century hermit Stephen of Muret who wrote:

'It shows admirable knowledge, and is very pleasing to God, when a man who is involved in an evil enterprise restrains himself from evil. It can be done like this. If a knight is setting out on an expedition for the sake of his secular lord, to whom he cannot refuse obedience, if he wishes to be faithful to God let him first speak thus in his heart: "Lord God, I will go on this expedition but I promise that I shall be your knight there, wanting nothing in it except to be obedient to you, to eliminate evil and to seek after what is good on every occasion as much as I can."'

Meanwhile Church-led Peace of God movements spread across France; and the knightly *milites* submitted to this new discipline with remarkable ease, probably because it offered Church recognition of their new status.

Greater wealth also enabled the knights to develop their own code of 'chivalry' and to patronise *trouveres* and *troubadours*. The 12th century is sometimes still seen as the golden age of chivalry when the Church was able to control the new power of the knights, but it was rarely seen this way at the time.

The castle of Saissac near Carcasonne is a typical small southern castle, *built in the 13th century. (Author's photograph)*

War could be appallingly savage, even against fellow Christians, and King Louis VI's execution of the defenders of Crécy-sur-Serre in 1115 was merely one example of terror tactics. Nor were 12th century knights' ladies such delicate flowers, for there were plenty of examples of fierce *châtelaines* defending castles while their husbands were away. Not until the 13th century did the three forces seeking to influence the knight's conscience—feudal values, religion, and women—lead to that 'chivalry' still regarded as typical of medieval Europe. A requirement to please the ladies had been added late in the 12th century and as the cult of Courtly Love spread, 'amorousness' became another chivalric virtue. Only the increased savagery and the involvement of more non-combatants which characterised 14th and 15th century warfare at last made this noble set of ideals irrelevant.

Mercenaries and infantry

Mercenaries fought in French armies in the late 10th century and by the 11th the term *soldeier* or paid warrior was common. The use of such troops within

Mould for the 'Seal of Raymond de Mondragon', 12th century. Here a knight from the Rhône valley is shown in reverse, wearing a mail hauberk with mail chausses on his legs. His helmet is of a type probably developed from the 11th century form seen in the Atlantic Bible. (Bib. Nat., Cab. des Medailles, Paris)

the Royal Domain steadily increased as the crown accepted money instead of military service. The oldest surviving Royal Accounts for 1202–3 show that a town paid three *livres* (pounds) in lieu of a fully equipped warrior, while a mercenary knight himself earned seven *sous* per day. Only along the borders of his Domain did the king insist on maintaining effective militias. Fortunately the Île de France, the heart of the Royal Domain, was one of the richest areas in France and could pay for the king's wars as he extended his authority. Royal mercenaries became, in fact, a readily available and ruthless army which included many skilled specialists. Most seem to have come from outside the kingdom, from Imperial Brabant, Hainault, the western parts of Germany and from Navarre in the south. Others came from the County of Flanders which, though within the French kingdom, was culturally close to Brabant and Hainault (these three counties are now western-central Belgium). Such forces enabled the king to mount longer sieges than would be possible with the 40 days' service of a feudal hosting.

Increasing specialisation was a feature of French armies in the early 13th century, paid mercenaries now including armoured knights, mounted sergeants, mounted archers (who would actually have fought on foot) and various other infantry, some enlisted under long contracts. Unlike other mercenaries, the paid knights normally bought their own equipment and war-horses. A wide social gulf also developed between knights who held land and those mercenary knights who did not. Nevertheless a successful mercenary leader could rise to prominence under the king's protection, some becoming *castellans* of royal castles or *baillis* of royal provinces. *Baillis* played a particularly important role under King Philip II Augustus (1180–1223), some having been poor knights while others were merchants' sons and other townsfolk.

Mercenary *sergeants*, both cavalry and infantry, were naturally cheaper than mercenary knights, though mounted *sergeants* with three or four *sous* per day still got four times as much as the *marescallus equorum* horse-master in charge of the squires. Infantry *sergeants* received nine *deniers* per day, slightly more than a *constable* in charge of a militia unit. The mounted *sergeants* also provided King Philip Augustus with his mace-armed cavalry bodyguard at the battle of Bouvines. In 1231 a cavalry *sergeant* was expected to have three horses (a *destrier* war-horse, a *palfrey* for riding and a baggage animal), as did a knight. By the late 13th and early 14th centuries *sergeants*, both cavalry and infantry, formed the bulk of French royal armies, while even the troops of leading barons included many such professionals. Though scorned by the aristocratic élite and with their most effective weapons often condemned by both knights and Church, the usefulness of such infantry was recognised by all. There was even some professional respect between mercenary knights and infantry but not, of course, any social contact.

Among the earliest mercenary infantry were the Brabançons, most of whom came from the County of Brabant in modern Belgium. They earned a considerable reputation from the mid-12th to early 13th centuries in siege operations, for their speed of marching and their ferocity against civilians. Most fought with long spears or pikes and formed a defensive rather than offensive force in open battle. Some had helmets and mail hauberks but the majority wore 'leather armour'—probably quilted leather *gambesons*—but these Brabançons declined in favour of crossbow-armed infantry in the 13th century. Other names given to 12th century infantry mercenaries were *cottereaux* or *coterelli*, perhaps referring to their short tunics, and *triaverdini*, whose meaning remains unclear.

King Richard I of England was said to have introduced the crossbow to France in 1185, but this was obviously untrue and probably reflected his more effective use of such weapons. Genoese from Italy and Gascons from the Spanish-influenced southwest of France were among the earliest professional crossbowmen, while crossbows remained more common in southern Europe than the north throughout the 12th century. Meanwhile crossbowmen were relatively well paid in the armies of King Philip Augustus: the few mounted crossbowmen received five *sous* per day, the infantry crossbowmen eighteen *deniers*. Mounted crossbowmen became increasingly important to the French kings during the 13th century while mounted archers, though still recorded in 1205, soon died out. Both operated as mounted infantry, actually fighting on foot. By the early 14th century it was Italian crossbowmen who were the most highly prized.

The first Master of Crossbowmen in the French king's service whose name we know was Thibaud de Montléard, who was arrested in 1230. By 1295 a French crossbowman was supposedly protected by a mail coif, a *bascinet* helmet and quilted tunic. He carried his bolts (arrows) in a quiver slung from a baldric and also had a sword, the total cost of such equipment being three *livres tournois*—a considerable sum.

Loot and ransom might have secured the future of those mercenaries who survived their hazardous trade, but many must have ended up as poor as they started. Perhaps it was from the ranks of the less successful that the 'champions' who fought on behalf of others in trial by battle were drawn. Such men were regarded as desperadoes on a level with prostitutes, but they remained part of the legal scene for centuries.

The distinction between mercenary and feudal infantry was not always clear. From the 10th to 12th centuries most foot soldiers were untrained rustic levies, but among the more effective were javelin-throwers and archers. In open battle 11th century

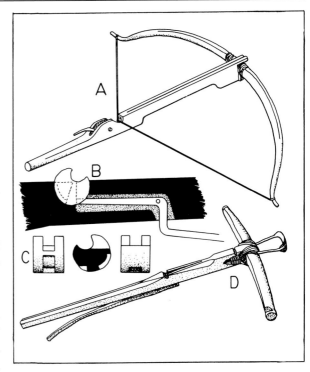

(A) Reconstruction of a small 11th century hunting crossbow found at Colletiére in the Dauphiné. The stock and bow are both about 50cm long. The trigger is on the top and the string is released by the upwards motion of a small peg. (B) Section through the simple nut and trigger system used in 12th century crossbows. (C) Front, sectional and rear views of a typical 12th–13th century crossbow release nut. (D) A large 14th century crossbow, perhaps to be rested on a castle wall, with the bowstring removed. Even at this date the string is still released by the upwards movement of a small peg. (Landesmus., Zurich)

infantry used hand bows, spears and long pikes while the trained *servientes*, predecessors of the *sergeants*, could still hold a defensive position against cavalry. In fact unarmoured cavalry faded from the military scene as archers were increasingly brought into play. By the early 12th century ranks of armoured infantry protected the archers while ranks of foot soldiers, stiffened by dismounted knights, could use their spears as pikes. The most common 12th century infantry formation seems to have been in straight ranks, preferably behind a protective ditch, with spiked calthrops scattered ahead. Yet such tactics remained vulnerable to flank attack and did little to undermine the knights' domination.

The rise of crossbows led to the virtual disappearance of simple bows as war weapons in France and no hand bows are recorded in surviving castle inventories from 1230 to the mid-14th century. On the other hand these listed an increasing number of various crossbows, one bow to 50 quarrels, bolts or arrows being a typical proportion. Other specialised infantry weapons from the mid-13th century onwards were *faussarts* (perhaps early *falchions*), large axes and maces.

At the same time trained infantry were steadily growing in importance, playing a major military role by the late 13th century. New types of foot soldiers were also emerging, including the French *bidauts* light skirmishers of 1302. The fame of the Flemings in siege warfare had been known for centuries, but they were also developing effective tactics in open battle. Flemish pikemen supported by men wielding *goedendags*, massive wooden maces, certainly came into their own in the early 14th century by overthrowing the pride of French chivalry at the battle of Courtrai. The *goedendag*, though mostly associated with Flemish cities like Brugge and Gent, was also used in northern France.

Militias

A lot is known about the recruitment and organisation of militia infantry. The old Carolingian concept that all free landholding men could be called upon to fight had not died out, but the obligations of the common folk had declined considerably by the 12th century. Duties excluded *ost* and *chevauchée*, the peasantry being regarded as 'rear vassals' only to be called out under a general *arrière ban*. A general levy of 1124 against a German invasion included many peasant *pedites* infantrymen, but in case of war between a nobleman and the king, commoners were excused from following their lord. Other obligations of ordinary people involved the building and repair of fortifications.

No serious effort seems to have been made to limit the carrying of weapons until the second half of the 12th century, though only in the towns would some men have been wealthy enough to possess proper arms. The waggons that the countryside could supply often seem to have been more important than the warriors; but in 1284 the abbot of St. Maur-des-

'Charlemagne's troops sleeping', c.1218. Here the kite-shaped shields are of a shorter late 12th century form. An interesting feature is the rigid facemasks on the helmets. (Roland Window, in situ Chartres Cathedral; author's photograph)

Fosses was able to summon a respectable force from the Abbey's estates: the 12 men who owned 60 pounds or more appeared with a mail hauberk, *chapel-de-fer* helmet and sword or *couteau* dagger; 53 men owning 30 pounds or more came with various types of quilted *gambeson*, *chapel-de-fer* and sword or dagger; those with ten pounds or more came only with a *chapel-de-fer* and sword or dagger, while those having less than ten pounds turned up with a bow, arrows and a dagger.

Merchants had always travelled heavily armed but, as trade expanded in the 13th century, most settled down to run their affairs from offices. Urban militias were rarely mentioned in northern France before the middle of the 12th century, though they may have existed. The need for the rising urban *communes* to have troops as well as adequate finances and political self-control to protect themselves against surrounding feudal forces was obvious. Most emerged in the mid-12th century, when they played a vital role against foreign invasion, and they became even more prominent under King Philip II Augustus.

The seals of most urban communes were warlike and showed towers, an armoured man or group of warriors. The military obligations of communes were now clear, their charters laying down precisely what duties were and were not owed to the local lord or his representative the *sénéchal*. These also specified where the militias should serve and for how long. Such charters listed the numbers of *sergeants* and waggons a town must supply, though these were increasingly replaced by money payments. Even so, many 12th and 13th century French townsmen spent a lot of time soldiering. A wide-ranging list of city, town and abbey obligations under Philip II Augustus totalled 7,695 *sergeants* and 138 carts, plus 11,693 *livres parisis* (Parisian pounds) from those who paid instead. At the same time it was getting more difficult

for the king to raise feudal levies through his great vassals. Under Louis IX, for example, the barons often refused to levy troops from their own people, arriving at the muster with the smallest possible following and returning home immediately their 40 days were up.

Under such circumstances the crown turned to

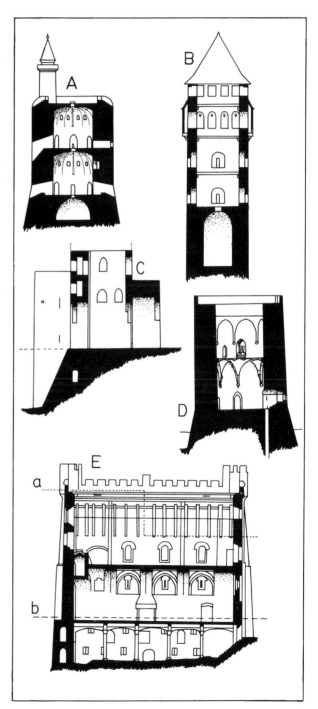

(A) Tour de Constance, the earliest part of the defences of Aigues-Mortes, built in 1241–50. The upper battlements were rebuilt in the 17th century. (B) Right-bank tower on the fortified Pont Valentre at Cahors, started in 1308. (C) Porte Saint-Jean at Provins, 13th century. (D) Isolated tower built at Villeneuve-sur-Yonne by King Philip Augustus, early 13th century. The upper part is now lost. (E) Castle of the Counts of Flanders, Gent; below line 'b' built before 1180; above line 'b' the donjon of c.1180; above line 'a' 19th century restoration.

and was cancelled ten years later. Nevertheless there was a thorough reorganisation under King Philip V in 1317, with the old 'rear vassals' being drawn back into the system. Each town or province was again responsible for providing men, equipment and leaders, all to be placed under regional commanders approved by the king. The most detailed information about the organisation of such militias comes from Flanders and its neighbours. Here late 13th century militias were generally organised around craft guilds, each providing 'constabularies' of both fighting men and servants led by their own commanders and equipped at the guild's expense. The richest citizens fought as cavalry but the majority, of course, still served on foot.

Early militias, while enforcing the 11th century Peace of God, acted in the king's name though often being led by local abbots. The growing wealth of some 12th century towns enabled their militias to be well equipped, but citizen soldiers remained part-timers with little training who generally needed the support of knights or mercenaries. Yet their morale was often good. In 1177 the peasants of the Lâon region rose against a bishop who was their lord. They summoned the militias of Crépi, Vaili and other communes to their aid, while the bishop summoned those of Lâon town, Soissons and the Abbey of St. Médard together with his feudal forces. A brief battle took place near the little River Ailette, but the peasant militias had taken up a position on a grassy plain with their flanks open to cavalry attack and as a result were quickly beaten.

Nevertheless militias were probably more effective than the aristocratic chroniclers would have us believe. Not only could they defend fortified walls, but at the battle of Bouvines in 1214 they were arrayed under their own banners directly in front of the king, forming a defensive block around which the cavalry could manoeuvre. We also know that the opposing Imperial infantry, including Flemings and Brançones, had pikes longer than French cavalry lances, while others had hooked spears to pull French horsemen from their saddles. Most operations outside their own walls seem, however, to have been 'police' duties. In 1233 19 communes successfully put down a rebellion in the Beauvais area. The Flemish uprising in the early 14th century was largely based upon militia forces, and their staggering

'David and Goliath', La Charité Psalter, *Loire region, late 12th century. Goliath wears the old-fashioned equipment often given to 'infidels' in medieval manuscripts,* *though such short-hemmed, short-sleeved mail hauberks would also have been issued to sergeants. (Ms. Harl. 2895, f.51v, Brit. Lib., London)*

the towns for troops. In 1253 nine towns of the Massif Central region provided over 3,000 *sergeants*. Half a century later most wealthy citizens payed to be exempted service, this money being used to hire professionals who were probably more useful. During a military emergency of 1303–4 the crown tried to turn payment for exemption into a regular tax from both nobles and commoners, only serfs being exempted, but this caused widespread resentment victory over French knighthood at Courtrai was not their only success in open battle. Flemish militias won two of the four main clashes (Courtrai, 1302, and Arques, 1303) while losing the others (Mons-en-Pévèle, 1304, and Cassel, 1328).

The equipment available to militiamen varied according to the wealth of the commune, city or region. Generally speaking urban militias were better off than rural ones. Body armour was very rare in the 12th century, though wealthy citizens might serve as armoured cavalry. Mail hauberks became more common in the 13th century, but the majority still fought in quilted 'old and blackened' *gambesons*. Small round buckler shields appear in late 13th and early 14th century sources, but some experts suggest that sword-and-buckler fighting was more of a sport than a war skill. Surviving documents from French-speaking Liège, beyond the French frontier, specify the arms possessed by certain citizens. For example, in 1281 Simon Stourmis owned a full mail hauberk; while in 1311 a clerk named Jean Fabri had a smaller mail *haubergeon*, a perhaps metal-plated leather *cuirie* and a *bascinet* helmet with mail *aventail*. Many if not most of the guild-based militias of French Flanders are also known to have worn some kind of uniform in the 13th and 14th centuries, probably simple surcoats of a specified colour.

Engineers and commissariat

Although some cities were famous for the siege skills of their miners and sappers, professional engineers could also be counted among the ranks of mercenaries, coming to particular prominence under King Philip II Augustus. Those operating Simon de Montfort's massive stone-throwing *trebuchets* a few years later earned 21 *livres* per day—a huge sum even if it was divided among several men. Under Philip Augustus *minarii* who used picks to undermine enemy walls got 18 *deniers* per day, and pioneers, masons and labourers 15 *deniers*.

Such auxiliary services were generally regarded as part of an army's commissariat which, by the late

Effigy of Raoul II de Beaumont, c.1220. This is one of the earliest military effigies in Europe and it portrays the Vicomte fully mailed but without a surcoat. His helmet is of the tall domed type with a rim band and a substantial nasal. (Musée Archéologique, Le Mans, Cliché Musées du Mans)

12th century, was highly organised. Philip II of France's military bureaucrats listed the equipment in each royal castle. In Normandy, for example, Pacy-sur-Eure had 26 'stirrup' crossbows, 38 of the 'two foot' kind and five larger crossbows *ad tornum*, 11 mail hauberks, 23 'doubled' helmets (either with a mail coif or including a close-fitting *cervelière*), and 23 ordinary helmets. Little Illiers L'Eveque only had two stirrup crossbows. Arsenals in fortified towns were equally varied. Chinon had four crossbows *ad tornum*, three 'two foot' crossbows, 13 'stirrup' crossbows and 22 others 'in the hands of Pierre de Saint-Giles' (later recorded as governor of nearby Langeais); 2,000 quarrels for the crossbows *ad tornum*, 10,000 for the 'two foot' type, 33,000 for the 'stirrup' crossbows; 20 'sharp blades' and three 'crosses' (meanings unclear); 60 large shields and 30 smaller shields; 400 cords for *petraria* stone-throwing machines, 11 large siege engines of various kinds including one *petraria turquesia* (an early form of *espringal*); six large waggons and 26 smaller types, stores of food and wine; plus four 'doubled' helmets, 26 mail coifs and ten *colerias* (protections for the neck

and shoulders). At the other end of the scale was Lyons-le-Forêt with only five mail hauberks, four smaller mail shirts and nine helmets.

The provision of carts was a vital part of the commissariat, one being needed for every 40 or 50 *sergeants* under Philip Augustus. Tents were also important. The names given to various types suggest strong Arab-Islamic influence, either through Spain or via the Crusades, and the way they were made would support such an idea.

Horses

Another area in which France, like the rest of Western Europe, gained much from contact with the Muslim world was that of horse-breeding. A lot of nonsense surrounds the medieval knight's war-horse or *destrier*; in fact horses need physical weight to pull weight, not to carry it, for which they merely need strength. The medieval European war-horse was not a cold-blooded 'heavy horse', but what would be considered a Cob, a rare breed that now survives most obviously in the Suffolk Cob and the Punch. Only towards the later Middle Ages and Renaissance, with the adoption of massive plate armour, might war-horses have taken on some of the characteristics of the modern Percheron and Ardennes breeds. *Destriers* had been known since the late 10th century. Information from a few centuries later indicates that they were trained to walk but not trot, which would have been painful for an armoured rider in the medieval 'peaked' saddle, and only at the last moment would they increase speed, charging at a slow canter rather than a gallop.

While these *destriers* were then, and would now be, regarded as 'cold blooded', the whole question of 'hot' and 'cold' blood is still widely misunderstood. There is no genetic basis for the distinction, which reflects temperament and the regions in which various breeds originated. Cob-like horses were abundant throughout medieval Europe in areas of good grass and clover. In earlier times Roman cavalry horses had more in common with those of the nomadic Scythian peoples of southern Russia, these

Ivory chess knight, south French, 12th century. Note the framed helmet with a substantial rim, perhaps intended to show an early *form of brimmed chapel-de-fer. (Bargello Mus., Florence; author's photograph)*

having the appearance of a larger form of Arabian horse. Meanwhile the ancient riding horse of the Middle East seems to have been the ancestor of the modern Barb. The quality of Western European war-horses clearly declined following the fall of the Roman Empire, and most horses available to Charlemagne and his successors were not very impressive, failing against the invading Magyars on their tough steppe ponies. Nevertheless the old breeds survived in the south where, in the early medieval period, they seem to have been similar to those of the Arabs on the southern side of the Mediterranean.

Until the 13th or 14th centuries the Middle Eastern or Arab-Islamic riding tradition (as distinct from Turco-Islamic Central Asian tradition) was basically the same as that of the Romans, though with the addition of stirrups and more developed saddles. Like the medieval knights whom they influenced, Arab warriors only mounted their war-horses immediately before a battle, otherwise travelling on

City walls of Carcassonne. These were built shortly after the Albigensian Crusade. Note the outer *moat, doubled circuit walls and tall half-rounded towers. (Author's photograph)*

mules, donkeys or camels as the medieval knight travelled on his *palfrey*. In fact the medieval Western riding tradition developed out of both the ancient Roman and the more recent Arab-Islamic fashions. The Western war-saddle, though it eventually differed from the lighter versions of the Middle East, also developed from a padded, wood-framed saddle supported on felt pads which had been brought to Europe by the Arabs during the early Middle Ages. The same was true of elaborate forms of curb bit which, though known to the Romans, had died out in most of Europe.

Where the breeding of war-horses was concerned the medieval French had almost everything to learn from the Muslims—and here the Arabs contributed a new attitude instead of reviving something lost since

Roman times. Unlike their predecessors, the Arabs had, since pre-Islamic times, bred for quality rather than quantity. The first recorded Arab veterinary manual dated from AD 785 while the artificial insemination of mares was known by at least 1286. Arabian horses were imported via Spain as early as the 9th century and, perhaps as a result of the first Crusades, more powerful horses of Byzantine or Persian type reappeared during the 12th century. This, of course, was a time when the largely French Crusaders were supposedly 'bowling over the Saracens on their smaller ponies'. Arab influence can also be found in the terminology of medieval French horse breeding, where the word *bardot* (the mixed offspring of a stallion and she-ass) derived from the Arabic *birdhawn* meaning draught or pack horse.

The most immediate source of influence upon French horse breeding was Muslim Spain, where a famous stud had been established at Cordoba as early as the 8th century. It was in southern Spain that the famous Andalusian breed was developed. Basically descended from the North African Barb, which was also a foundation strain for the Arabian horse, the Andalusian was the first 'oriental' breed to be appreciated in Western Europe. William of Normandy had two at the battle of Hastings, and such so-called 'hot-blooded' horses were imported in large numbers from the late 11th century. Inevitably they had an impact not only on the character of the finest French war-horses but also, it seems, on the places where *destriers* were raised. The Perche region of southern Normandy later gave its name to the Percheron breed, but during the first half of the 12th century Count Rotrou III of Perche fought in the Spanish Reconquista, taking part in the capture of Saragossa and Tudela. Could Count Rotrou have brought back the horses which made Perche an important breeding centre and which ultimately sired the Percherons?

By the late 12th century, when a *Chanson de Geste* called the *Couronnement de Louis* was written, the ideal knight had quite a train of animals in tow. According to the *Couronnement* these consisted of his *destrier*, a *roncin* pack horse, a *palfrey* riding horse, a mule and another beast of burden. The *destrier* was naturally the most valuable, but the *palfrey* was also a specially trained animal: it was a 'pacer', a type of horse now mostly seen at dressage events. Its gait of 'pacing' was much more comfortable for its rider than trotting, particularly over long distances, but it was unnatural and had to be taught.

'Siege of Carcassonne by Simon de Montfort's Crusaders', early 13th century relief carving. The defenders have a crossbow and man-powered mangonel while many attackers wear flat-topped 'great helms'. (in situ Cathedral, Carcassonne)

THE ARMIES OF SOUTHERN FRANCE

The history of the French south or Midi differed from that of the north. During the 10th century the Counts of Toulouse had risen in power and there had been a considerable militarisation of the area; then, in the 11th century, these great nobles started to lose control, many of their peace-keeping functions falling to the Church. Meanwhile the new military class of *milites* was emerging. They were still of lowly status in the late 10th century, serving as full- or part-time warriors to the local *fideles* lords. By the middle of the 11th century, however, the *milites* had become a local power, though their relationship with the greater aristocracy was less 'feudal' than in northern France.

Until around 1180 the southern *milites* and more senior *caballarios* remained little more than pro-

fessional warriors, their status resting on their fighting skills alone. Yet during the 12th century they were also drawn into the courtly way of life so vividly reflected in the songs of the southern *troubadours*. While in the north there were four kinds of knight, in the south the *ministeriales* who lived in a lord's court hardly existed. There were, of course, great knights or lords as well as vassal knights who fought for the great as part of their feudal duties, but what set the south apart was a far larger proportion of mercenary knights on both short-term and long-term contracts.

Military relationships were more equal than those in the north, with lesser land- or castle-holding knights fighting for greater lords under *convenientiae* or 'treaties of mutual help' rather than as feudal vassals. The castles themselves were held under a variety of terms, many being owned as freehold property. There had always been more trade in the south and in the 12th century this expanded further, much of it centred upon Toulouse. Not all cities benefited equally and some were more warlike than others: Carcassonne, for example, had been a major military centre for centuries. Town-based knights were another feature, often dominating the cities along with richer merchants at a time when such towns were winning more independence.

From the mid-12th century feudal fiefs without castles also appeared in the deep south, while feudal rights over markets or tolls could be more important than those over land, as they brought in more money. Even in the 11th century it had been common for people to be given land in return for rents rather than military services. Such estates were often not hereditary, returning to the original lord on the death of the holder. In fact feudal duties and castles did not form the basis of the southern social order, as in the north, but resulted from an administrative system strongly rooted in the Roman past. One result of the southern way of doing things was that a large part of the population could claim 'noble' status by the 13th century, even if they held little or no land. In 1259 in the small region around Agen, for example, there were 150 *domicelli*, the lowest ranking members of the knightly class, in addition to higher ranking *milites* and *barones*.

Relaxation and realism

Not only were southern warriors organised in a different way, but there was a different attitude to warfare and the military way of life. Urban knights happily took part in money-making commerce while living in fortified town houses and holding *estager* fiefs within the walls. The *chevalier a coite* may have been a less militarised urban reserve or might simply have been another form of service owed by urban knights. A more common method of organisation was the *maisnade* which seems to have consisted of a lord's kinfolk, though even so such *maisnade* forces were often reinforced by mercenaries. There was little

IONISIVS

'Knight of the Clement family receiving the sacred French banner from St. Denis'. This warrior has typical 13th century arms and armour including a long sword-of-war. (Stained-glass window, in situ Chartres Cathedral; author's photograph)

idealisation of knightly 'glory' in southern France, which remained suspicious of what were seen as barbaric northern French ideas. The chivalric ideals of the north were rarely reflected in the south, nor did tournaments become popular. Even the term *adober*, to 'dub' a knight, continued to mean 'equip with proper military gear' as it had done in the 11th century, rather than referring to some mystical ceremony.

Instead the south evolved its own more peaceful ideals of Courtly Love which, strongly influenced by Muslim and Christian Spain, then spread northwards to 'tame' the ferocious warriors across the Loire. Meanwhile the better-educated knightly class of the south, along with the similarly literate merchants, were more open to new ideas. Unfortunately for the distinctive civilisation of the Midi, these included religious heresies such as that of the Cathars which took root in the south. It was supported by nobles as well as knights, and would lead to a full-scale northern French Crusade in the 13th century.

The military equipment of the south differed only in detail from that of northern France, as is shown in a description written by Arnaut Guilhem de Marsan in the 1170s:

'Have a good horse and I will tell you what kind. One that is swift running and apt for arms. Take this one at once and then your armour, lance, sword and hauberk with its surcoat. Let the horse be well tested and not a poor one, and put on it a good saddle and a bridle and a really fine peitral [breast-strap or front part of a horse armour] so that nothing is unsuitable, and have the saddle-cloth made with the same emblem as the saddle and the same colour as is painted on the shield, and the pennon on the lance in the same way. Have a pack-horse ready to carry your doubled hauberk and your armament held high so that they appear more fine, and always have the squires close by.'

The status of the southern squire also differed. In the 12th century the *escudiers* remained non-noble military servants. They looked after their masters' horses, saddlery and armour, led his *destrier*, took messages, ran errands and foraged on campaign. Squires might also have guarded the baggage train, while those of slightly higher rank served at table. The term *escudier* could overlap with that of *sirven* and *donzel*. *Sirvens* were numerous in the fortified

Angers Castle, built around 1228, lacks a central keep. Instead it consists of a curtain wall with numerous close-spaced towers. The striped decoration was probably inspired by Syrian architecture seen by French Crusaders. (Author's photograph)

towns and may have been comparable to the northern *sergeants*, while *donzels*, though often of noble birth, also acted as attendants or servants for the *cavalers* knights. Thirteenth century references to the *donzels* describe them fighting in full knightly armour or serving at table, helping their knight to wash and put on his armour rather than looking after his horses. Nevertheless it is unclear whether the *donzel* was an aspiring knight like the northern *juvene*, or was from a poor knightly family that had slipped down the social scale. During the late 12th century the status of the *escudiers* was also changing, and by the end of the 13th they were expected to fight, though remaining lightly armed. They still had little hope of becoming knights, but were advised to be 'clean and neat' even if they could not afford the latest fashions. Living in a knight's household, such squires were also dependent on him for pay.

A lack of cohesion on the part of southern military élites has often been blamed for their defeat during the Albigensian Crusade, and this did play a major role in the collapse of the southern military system. On the other hand southern forces often fought successfully, and they continued to do so after the Albigensian Crusade brought the Midi under northern control. Meanwhile southern France was divided between provinces ruled by the French crown and those which remained under the English as a theoretical vassal of the French. Here the defence of Gascony against the invading armies of Philip the Fair in 1294–8 largely fell to local Gascon knights, mercenaries and *sergeants* with only a few English troops taking part. Bayonne remained a centre of pro-English feeling, and the Gascon nobility certainly did not deserve the reputation for unreliability later given them.

Despite the importance of paid *soudadiers* in southern France, the distinction between mercenaries and vassals remained blurred. Less prestigious mercenaries included barely civilised mountain men from both sides of the Pyrenees. Gascons, Navarrese and Basques remained in demand as infantry from the 12th to 14th centuries, and their most characteristic weapons were a pair of heavy javelins or *dards* which they used 'in the manner of the wild Irish'. Others fought as archers, but it was the *dardiers* who most successfully harried and ambushed columns of invading northern French troops during the Albigensian Crusade. Aragonese from the eastern end of the Spanish Pyrenees also fought as mercenaries from the late 12th century. Some were knights or light cavalry but the most feared were *almogavers* (Arabic *al mughawir*, 'raiders') armed with spears or crossbows.

Less seems to be known about military engineers in southern France, despite the advanced nature of siege warfare in the Midi. One Gascon *magister ingeniorum*, however, was so respected that he was knighted in 1254 and went on to serve the Count of Savoy.

Militias

Militias also played a major role in southern warfare. Urban forces recruited from the *borzeis* burghers may even have been more important than they were in the

'Herod's guards', south French relief carving, early 13th century. The mailed warriors wear separate mail coifs while the quillons of the swords appear to be slightly curved. (In situ facade of Church of St. Trophime, Arles; author's photograph)

north, defending their fortified towns with hand bows, axes, *guisarmes* and large rocks during the 12th century. On campaign they were described by unsympathetic *troubadours* as escorting supply waggons armed with bows and carrying horns or pipes, while on raids they poisoned the enemy's wells. If captured, a *borzeis* or *sirven* militiaman might have a hand or foot cut off, while a captured knight lost only an ear or nose!

A breakdown of law and order in the mid-12th century led to a revival of the peace movement in the County of Toulouse, and once again the Church played a leading role, organising 'episcopal militias' or *communia* under local bishops. Meanwhile townsfolk paid an unpopular *tallage* tax for the upkeep of their walls, while the Order of Templars established a police force to protect the peasants in return for grain from each village. When militias did catch up with troublemakers they seemed well able to deal with them, as when the men of Limoges routed a band of

'Defeat of Moabites by Israelites', Maciejowski Bible, Paris c.1250. Both sides are similarly armed though great helms are only worn by the Israelites. Note the use of a dagger by one horseman, the axe of a foot soldier, the quilted gambesons with massive collars of two infantrymen and two different types of chapel-de-fer. (Pierpont Morgan Lib., New York)

marauding Brabançons at Easter 1192. The difficulty of dealing with banditry led to local systems of law enforcement, which in turn led to the growth of democratic local assemblies where citizens had to be consulted on all military matters. Most such assemblies were swept away by the Albigensian Crusade, when the Papal Legate also took over existing policing structures for use against heretics.

Nevertheless, militias survived the Albigensian Crusade. In 1286 the 'total community of Agenais' swore to help England's King Edward I in his quarrel with the French crown. A citizen army had already crushed troublesome Gascon nobles in 1255, while in French-ruled regions Philip the Fair called up

23

The Pont Valentre, built in 1308, is the most famous fortified bridge in France. It is protected by three tall towers. (Author's photograph)

militias almost every year after war broke out in 1294. Such armies would be summoned in late spring and ordered to meet at an agreed spot in summer; they then marched as far north as Rheims and Arras or to the closer frontier with English Gascony.

Even when militias served within their own towns they were liable for a complex array of different duties. In their heyday such duties included *gach* or *gag* (equivalent to the northern *guet*), meaning guarding the ramparts; and *reyregach* or *estialgach* (the northern *arrière-guet*), meaning policing the streets, checking the guards upon the walls and confiscating the weapons of those found asleep. Both *gach* and *reyregach* were normally performed at night, while *garde* or *garde des portes* was daytime duty at the city gates. In Bayonne in 1315 each married man had to appear in person once a week on pain of prison or a fine. Citizens were normally organised on a rota basis, being summoned at nightfall by a bell or trumpet. There were two watches per night, each under *capitans* who were generally outsiders over whom the urban leaders had little control. In a strategic town like Bayonne even the role of mayor was primarily military. Some important cities had royal garrisons while others recruited mercenaries, particularly at harvest time, though most relied on their own inhabitants. Each family normally possessed a number of weapons, and was liable for a fine if they failed in their duties.

If a town was attacked then all able-bodied citizens from the ages of 18 to 60, including women, were mobilised. The women carried weapons, food and drink to the men, and were even helped by children, priests and monks if the situation got serious. Only beggars and foreigners were excused, on security grounds. Noblemen resident within the town seem to have avoided *gach* and *garde*, perhaps because they served in the *reyregach* as a mounted reserve to reinforce a threatened section of wall. Such a reserve could also make sorties outside the walls. The defence of the gates remained, however, the most important element in the defences and was often under a full-time gatekeeper, who either led a band of the most reliable citizens or headed a unit of mercenaries.

An alarm would be raised by bells, banners, trumpets or beacons, and the term *efrei* described the citizens' full mobilisation in time of imminent danger. Militias would then be divided into small squads, five forming a company of about 50 men. If the town was attacked militiamen lined the walls, sometimes supported by their families, while archers and cross-bowmen manned loop-holes lower down the wall. Craftsmen were called up to repair damaged weapons, while *badas* or lookouts were posted on surrounding hills; at night these lookouts were replaced by *scotas* who listened for suspicious noises. Meanwhile the town leaders sent *messatges* (messengers) and *espias* (spies) to keep themselves informed of developments further afield.

If militias were summoned to serve in the army of the king or local lord their units seem to have been small, and these were probably selected on the basis of military skill. The bulk of militiamen who served outside their cities seem to have been poorer artisans who were paid for their services but they were generally led by a prominent citizen, consul or *capitan* while marching behind the town's banner and trumpeter. Once they joined the main army militia units were probably divided into smaller units and dispersed.

The equipment available to southern militias was as varied as that seen in the north. The mail hauberks demanded of richer sailors in early 13th century Bayonne, and the quilted jerkin and iron hat expected

The 11th century
1: Northern French miles warrior
2: Southern French miles
3: Southern French peasant levy

A

First half 12th century
1: King Louis VI the fat
2: Seigneur of a castle
3: French militiaman, early 12th century

B

Second half 12th century
1: Spanish mercenary knight in service
   of English Gascony, c 1187–88
2: Southern French infantryman
3: Navarrese mercenary infantryman

C

The army of Philip Augustus, early 13th century
1: The Sire de Montfort, c 1215
2: Brabancon knight being armed, c 1225
3: French squire

D

The last Albigensian rising, mid-13th century
1: Southern French sergeant from Country of Foix
2: French royal knight
3: Southern French crossbowman from Bigone

The French invasion of Aragon,
late 13th century
1: French infantry sergeant
   from Toulouse
2: French military engineer
3: Aragonese light cavalryman
   of Cardona family

F

Battle of Courtrai, 1302
1: French knight
2: Senior Flemish militiaman
3: Flemish urban militia crossbowman

G

Knightly dubbing ceremony, c 1328
1: French baron
2: French squire
3: French knight

H

of the rest, probably mirrored the armour used by Bayonne's militia. Information from the late 13th century Customs of Lectoure near Agen indicates that citizens equipped themselves, every household possessing at least a sword, lance, shield and padded coif; whether this reflected reality or was an ideal remains unclear, as weapons were expensive. In time of peace citizens also tended to sell their equipment, since the carrying of arms in public was often banned, while in time of crisis armament might be seized by the town bailiffs to equip professional troops. A richer town could, on the other hand, buy arms in bulk if danger threatened and then distribute them to its most reliable citizens. Southern towns generally had stores of weaponry but, like those in the north, these could be small. Nevertheless an Ordnance of 1317 insisted that all arsenals be guarded by royal officers.

'Effigy of Jean d'Alluye' from Abbey of Clarté-Dieu, Touraine, mid-13th century. The knight's relatively light sword is in a scabbard attached to the sword-belt in an unusual manner. (Cloisters Mus., New York; author's photograph)

STRATEGY AND TACTICS

Strategy and tactics were not as highly developed in Western Europe as they were in Byzantine and Muslim armies but they still showed planning on the part of military commanders. In France broad strategy was perhaps more important than battlefield tactics, but this reflected limitations of communications and control rather than any short-sightedness on the part of commanders. From the 11th to 13th centuries military leaders tended to avoid major battles, whose risks usually outweighed the advantages. Instead warfare in France, where the art of fortification was quite advanced, mostly consisted of raids to inflict economic damage, defence against raids, sieges, and the holding of territory thus won. Such aspects of medieval warfare have too often been neglected by historians who look for battles as 'turning points' in history. Consciously or otherwise most medieval commanders followed the advice of the late Roman theoretician Vegetius on the fighting of battles—namely, don't!

For the invader good lines of communications were essential, as were the hordes of camp followers who kept his troops supplied. The greatest fears would be disease within the ranks and enemy efforts to cut communications. Meanwhile the defenders would block roads, demolish bridges, attack the raiders as they dispersed ever wider in search of food, and try to cut their retreat. Both sides needed information about the loyalty of the enemy's cities. The French, for example, were aware of dissension within the Angevin (English) empire in France, and used this in various successful conquests. The strategic importance of the lower Seine River, which ran from Paris through English-held Normandy, was fully understood by Philip Augustus, who put enormous effort into recovering it for the French crown. A quotation from the early 13th century *Chansons des Lorrains* described a march through enemy territory:

'The march begins. Out in front are the scouts and incendiaries. After them come the foragers whose job is to collect the spoils and carry them in the great baggage train. Soon all is in tumult. The peasants, having just come out of their fields, turn back uttering loud cries. The shepherds gather their flocks and drive them towards the neighbouring woods in hope of saving them. The incendiaries set the villages on fire and the foragers visit and sack them. The terrified inhabitants are either burned or led away with their hands tied to be held for ransom. Everywhere bells ring the alarm, a surge of fear sweeps over the countryside. Wherever you look you can see helmets glistening in the sun, pennons waving in the breeze, the whole plain covered with horsemen. Money, cattle, mules and sheep are all seized. The smoke billows and spreads, flames crackle. Peasants and shepherds scatter in all directions' (trans. E. B. Krehbiel).

This, then, was the reality of war in the 'Age of Chivalry', and there was little role here for the heavily armoured knight. Instead such campaigns depended on common soldiers who fought for plunder and profit. The growing strength of medieval fortifications meant that, throughout the 13th and early 14th centuries, warfare largely remained a matter of raids by relatively small forces lacking siege equipment. Defeat in a major battle could also open up whole provinces to enemy raids. This happened to the French after Courtrai when the victorious Flemings ravaged Artois, seizing almost ungarrisoned castles and trying to devastate the countryside. Only towns with professional troops, like Thérouanne with its small garrison of Italian mercenaries, could resist.

(A) Motte & Bailey castle at Peray, built for Robert II de Bellême in 1090–1100 as a defence against the Counts of Maine, plus a sectional view. (B) Circular donjon at Houdan, completed in 1137. (C) Windowless donjon at Boussac, one of the earliest stone castles in Berry. (D) Castle of Laval, showing the circular 12th century tower and other fortifications added in the 13th century. (E) Castle of Villandraut, built in a new Italian style in 1306–7. (F) Fortress of Foix on a steep rocky outcrop, showing the rectangular donjon and hall of the 12th century, a massive circular tower and additional walls from the 15th century, and outer defences from a later date.

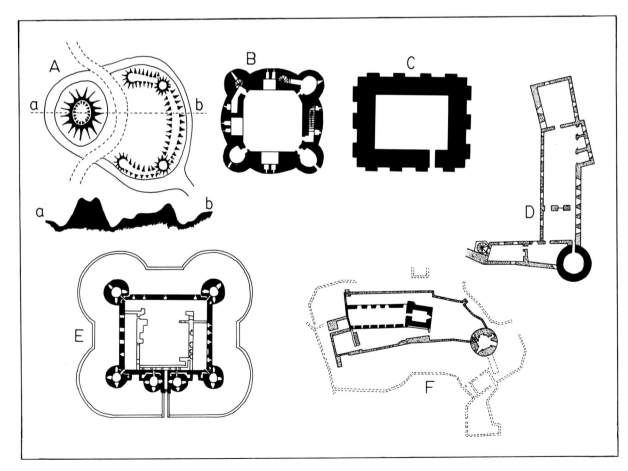

Defensive strategy was also carefully thought out. While the biggest medieval castles were mostly sited as bases for aggression, other fortifications served as refuges for a beaten force and as bases from which to attack an invader's supply lines. The 13th century saw a great multiplication of castles in France, particularly in English-ruled Gascony, which felt threatened by the French kings. Edward I of England also created a series of new *bastides* or fortified frontier towns.

On the other hand French armies had grown larger by the start of the 14th century when Philip the Fair faced war on two fronts, dealing with a major uprising in Flanders and maintaining garrisons along the Gascon frontier. Philip's forces may have reached 30,000 men, though a field army would only have ranged from 5,000 to 10,000. Peacetime garrisons could be nominal, such as the four horsemen and four infantrymen who 'defended' the city of Lille; while during a crisis that of Bordeaux rose to four *bannerets*, 23 knights, 227 squires and 192 *sergeants*, not counting the local militia. Cavalry could be summoned more quickly than infantry, but foot soldiers greatly outnumbered horsemen in almost all armies. Records for the small *bailliage* of Mâcon in eastern France show that in 1303–4 the militia were organised into nine *constabularies*, plus 100 professional *sergeants* and a handful of mercenary cavalry. A force operating out of Mâcon against Lyon, which lay within the German Empire until 1312, consisted of 17 knights and 113 other cavalrymen, plus 2,188 infantry—a proportion of 17 to 1.

Such regional armies would generally have been commanded by princes of the blood, counts and dukes who were close relatives of the king. These were also responsible for raising troops or the taxes with which to pay mercenaries within their own great *appanages* provinces. Princes of the blood were, however, rarely mentioned in the lists of men liable for military service because they themselves were responsible for administering such lists. Meanwhile the princes were expected to set an example of military leadership and loyalty to the crown.

Under Philip the Fair there was no permanent army; but there was a permanent command structure under a Royal Constable, two Marshals and a Master of the Crossbowmen in charge of infantry. These were Great Officers of the Crown and, though they

'Knight mounting his horse', Album of Villard de Honnecourt, French mid-13th century. The man's mail coif is thrown back revealing a linen coif worn beneath. His hauberk includes mail mittens but his chausses are in the old style exposing the rear of the legs. (Bib. Nat., Ms. Fr. 19.093, Paris)

were not full-time soldiers, they spent a great deal of time on military matters. Compared with the Constable and Marshals the Master of Crossbowmen was also a less political office. In war, positions of command above these officers went to princes of the blood, while in the south the noble *seneschals* or provincial governors also commanded regional armies. Lower in rank were lesser nobles who served as a matter of honour but rarely took part in more than three campaigns. Since cavalry and infantry forces generally had separate chains of command, presumably reflecting the much higher prestige of horsemen, problems of co-ordinating the movements of horse and foot were a common feature in most battles.

The typical raiding and siege warfare of the 11th

Church of Royat, early 13th century. Though considerably restored, this church still has the massive walls and crenellations typical of the fortified churches of central France. (Author's photograph)

to early 14th centuries also demanded military experts or specialists from garrison troops to engineers, crossbowmen, incendiaries and foragers. Most were infantry, the role of cavalry remaining reconnaissance, patrolling, escorting an army on the march and protecting foragers as they spread across enemy territory. Even though infantry had clearly declined in importance and skill by the beginning of this period, all-cavalry battles remained rare. From the late 11th century onwards it was normal for infantry to protect the horsemen, either by taking up positions ahead or by forming a 'box' around them. In battle such infantry were probably organised into several virtually autonomous formations.

The old view that medieval commanders had little tactical sense and that medieval warfare depended on the courage of individuals is almost certainly wrong. Successful Western European commanders were well aware of their limited ability to communicate orders once a battle had begun. If a major battle was risked they therefore took care to choose a strong position, arraying their troops to their best advantage and deciding upon points of attack or the actions of specific units before the fighting began. By the 13th century a widespread interest in Vegetius was also seen in France, new translations being made in which archaic Roman terms and concepts were replaced by 'modern' ones.

Among the earliest detailed descriptions of a French array is that of an army drawn up before King Louis VI in 1114. Here the *echelles* or squadrons formed larger units, the first supposedly of 60,000 men (a clearly inflated figure) from Rheims and Châlons, the second of men from Lâon and Soissons, the third from the Orléannais, Étampes, Paris and the Abbey of St. Denis, the fourth being followers of Thibaud de Chartres and Hughes de Troyes.

Ten years later Louis managed to gather a huge feudal army to face the Emperor Henry V of Germany near Rheims. This force, which so daunted Henry that he retired without a fight, consisted of an advance guard under the Duke of Burgundy and the Count of Nevers, a right wing under the Count of Vermandois, and a left consisting of men from Ponthieu, the Amiens area and Beauvais. The defensive centre was largely formed of militia infantry from Rheims-Châlons-Lâon-Soissons, Orleans-Étampes-Paris and Chartres-Blois-Brie-Troyes-Champagne, with a fourth section from Flanders-Aquitaine-Brittany-Anjou as a rearguard.

The battle of Bouvines, at which Philip Augustus defeated the combined armies of England and Germany in 1214, is sometimes regarded as a 'typical' medieval head-to-head confrontation, with each side hurling themselves into the fray with an equal lack of tactical thought. In reality both Philip and his foes put a lot of care into their initial dispositions. The battle of Muret, when Simon de Montfort's northern French Albigensian Crusaders defeated a largely Aragonese army from northern Spain, was one of those rare events, an all-cavalry clash—the foot soldiers of both sides were involved elsewhere or were too far away to take part. Nevertheless Peter II of Aragon still attempted to use local features such as small streams, dry gulleys and perhaps a marsh to protect his position. In fact these failed to stop three charges by De Montfort's three cavalry divisions which drove the front rank of Aragonese knights back into their second line of squires and eventually scattered Peter's men who were unsupported by infantry. De Montfort's foot soldiers then streamed out of a nearby town, where they had been besieged by the militiamen of Toulouse, to finish off the Aragonese wounded, while the northern French cavalry returned to slaughter the Toulousain militia. A final element in this battle, the troops of Count Raymond of Toulouse, had remained encamped on a nearby hill since their leader correctly regarded King Peter's tactics as faulty.

The armoured horseman was, in many ways, the main 'projectile' in the more open kinds of Western European warfare. Shock cavalry tactics of the 11th to 14th centuries were, however, essentially the same as those seen in all centuries. The psychological impact of massed cavalry upon infantry was at least as important as actual physical contact while the ranks of horsemen, advancing in very close formation though at no great speed, attempted to break through the enemy's line. Reserves were vital to such tactics, taking advantage of breaks to pass through and attack him from the rear. Flank attacks by cavalry, particularly against static infantry, were attempted when possible, while horsemen were also supposed to protect their own foot soldiers from such attacks.

The largest tactical unit in France was the *bataille*. This was made up of *conrois* which normally consisted of two or three very close-packed ranks of horsemen (ideally 20 to 24 men), the riders' stirrups supposedly touching those of their neighbours. In general the front rank of a 12th or 13th century *conrois* consisted of knights, the others of *sergeants*, while the still largely non-combatant squires brought up the rear. The smallest units were called *echielle* but it is unclear whether they acted as tactical formations or were administrative units. More sophisticated cone- or arrow-shaped cavalry formations were known in the 10th century Middle East and Byzantium, and in 14th century Spain, but were not recorded in France. Specifically light cavalry units were similarly almost unknown, although in the early 13th century the light horsemen of Catalonia had proved well able to cope with the heavy knights of an invading French army. French infantry were also organised into *batailles* by the early 14th century.

Encampments were similarly carefully organised. In the late 11th century these were often referred to as *hernerge* from the Old German term *heriberga*. The name for the night sentinels who guarded such camps, *escalguaite*, also came from Old German, as did *enguarde* outpost, *conrois* and *eschielle*—all in-

'Seal of John de Montfort', 1248. The horseman appears to have an early form of great helm while his horse has a chamfron to protect its head, as well as a full caparison. (Douët d'Arcq. no. D 713, Archives Nationales, Paris)

Lead pilgrim badge from the river Seine, late 13th or early 14th century. It probably represents St. George. (City Museum, Rouen; author's photograph)

'St. James of Compostella', 13th century statue. The patron Saint of Spain carries a sheathed sword with a new form of buckled sword-belt wrapped around it. (In situ Amiens Cathedral; author's photograph)

dicating a continuing link with the Carolingian period when German words had dominated much military terminology.

While infantry forces tried to anchor their flanks on obstacles such as woods, rivers or high ground, in open terrain where this was impossible they tended to adopt a 'crown' formation: its exact shape remains unknown, but the image suggests that it was 'spiky' all round. More is known about 12th to 14th century Flemish infantry, who formed up in a solid rectangular phalanx but adopted a circular formation if surrounded. Byzantine traditions, which dominated Western warfare until the 11th century, used infantry archers as skirmishers before a battle, to cover the army while it deployed and to protect its flanks. They were rarely formed into ranks, where javelin-armed infantry provided the main 'missile' element. In fact

it seems that crossbowmen, once they appeared in large numbers, inherited the tactical role of javelineers rather than hand-bow archers. By the late 12th century such crossbowmen often fought behind ranks of pikemen, being supported by loaders who spanned their crossbows and thus enabled them to maintain a respectable shooting rate. Meanwhile light infantry found a role in the 12th to 14th centuries when, armed with small shields and swords or heavier falchions, they formed up behind men with pikes, axes and other long-hafted weapons. Their task was to attack enemy cavalry if they threatened to break through, or to pursue them if they lost their cohesion. By the late 13th century casualties seem to have been much greater when fighting in northern France, perhaps because of the greater discipline of Flemish infantry militias, than in southern France where campaigns often took on the character of guerrilla warfare.

Medieval French flags and banners may not have been as developed as those in Byzantium and the Muslim countries, yet they played a role in battlefield identification and control. They also served as rallying points and indicated the direction of attack, often being stationed in or slightly ahead of the front rank. Another Western feature was the *cantador*, singer and speechmaker, who went ahead of an army to maintain its martial ardour, perhaps with extracts from favourite *Chansons de Geste*. Musical instruments such as the *buisine* trumpet, *corn* horn and *olifant* ivory horn, had also played a role since at least the 11th century, and the Flemings brought their use in battlefield control to a high degree by the early 14th century. Military drums were much less important in France, those that were mentioned often having names derived from Arabic (for example *tabor* and *nakerys*).

The evolution of the typical French medieval armoured horseman, with his couched lance, peaked saddle and straight-legged riding position, depended upon an earlier adoption of horseshoes and breast and crupper straps, most of which came from Central Asia. Stirrups were also important, though perhaps overemphasised, and they again originated in Asia. Stirrups were, in fact, essential when using a spear in the 'couched lance' manner locked between the chest and upper arm, but not for the effective use of sword, mace or horseman's axe.

The fully developed Western European 'jousting saddle' was known by the early 12th century, though the term *arcons*, referring to extensions to the rear of a saddle, had been recorded at least a generation earlier. In the fully developed peaked or jousting saddle these *arcons* wrapped around a rider's buttocks, making it very difficult to unseat him. On the other hand it was equally difficult for a rider to remount such a saddle if unhorsed. The curb bit, which gave a rider more immediate control over his horse, spread throughout Europe by the 14th century, having been reintroduced from the Islamic lands, but spurs had never fallen out of use since Roman times. In fact they remained unchanged throughout the early Middle Ages, only adopting a slightly curved outline in the late 12th century. The rowel spur with a spinning spiked wheel was first recorded in 13th century Russia and Byzantium, and did not become popular in France until the 14th.

The true couched lance appeared in the west in the mid-11th century, having been known in Byzantium for at least a hundred years, and the throwing of spears from horseback was probably abandoned in France by the late 11th century. During the 12th and 13th centuries the design of lances, shields and mail *hauberks* showed increasing concern for the penetrating power of lances which had increased with the couched technique. Contrary to a widespread misapprehension, the wings beneath the blades of 11th century cavalry spears were not suited to the couched lance technique and were not designed to prevent excessive penetration of a victim's body; rather, they were a hangover from early techniques in which a spear was held in both hands using thrusting and cutting motions. By the 12th century Western European cavalry lances were regarded as notably long, perhaps because the couched technique enabled a rider to hold his weapon well behind its point of balance. Late 12th century references to lances being 'laid upon the saddlebow' during a charge were probably poetic exaggerations, although the European peaked or jousting saddle did develop a remarkably high cantle to protect the rider's groin and abdomen.

In the early 11th century the *milites*' training was

'War between Angevins and Hohenstauffens', late 13th century wall painting. These crude pictures show a new style of conical great helm as well as small metal plates to protect knees and elbows. (In situ Tour Ferrande, Pernes-les-Fontaines; author's photograph)

much the same as that seen in Carolingian times; namely riding, fencing, throwing javelins, and using the spear or lance against a *quintaine* target. While the javelin faded out of use, the *quintaine* rose in importance from the 12th century onwards. Early tournaments also had a training role as participants normally took part in *conrois* units rather than as individuals.

Training in the use of the sword from horseback was, of course, also vital, as an unskilled man would be likely to hit his own horse or foot. On the other hand continued use of a baldric (shoulder belt) rather than a waist belt to carry a sword suggests that this weapon was of secondary importance to cavalry until the 12th century. A more massive 'sword of war'

came into use in France from around 1280. This was not, of course, a two-handed weapon but was a longer sword designed for cavalry use in which the blade was some 90 to 100cm long with a 15 to 20cm hilt. The earliest known medieval European fencing manual was written in Milan only a few years later, although this seemingly concentrated on the new so-called 'Italian grip' which permitted a more flexible cut-and-thrust fencing style using lighter swords. Such a fencing fashion originated in the Middle East and reached France in the early years of the 14th century. Meanwhile the dagger, which had been despised in France, also rose in importance.

Infantry warfare was divided between close-combat and missile weapons. The most important defensive weapon was the spear throughout the 11th to 13th centuries. Long-hafted war-axes were also prominent from the late 12th century and, as these grew in prestige, longer edged but lighter blades appeared. The bill, popular in both France and Italy, was probably descended from the German *beil* war-axe, but declined as heavier armour was introduced. The *glaive* is said by some to have been descended from the 'war scythe'—a farming implement converted into a weapon—and was used by peasant infantry or militias in France, Italy and southern Germany. The great length of such *glaives* was often noted, as was the fact that they had a point which could be thrust into a foe as well as an axe-like cutting edge. The *guisarme* was another long-bladed, long-hafted war-axe used in the 13th century, while the more obscure 13th century French *vouge* may also have been a form of long-hafted axe. Winged or flanged maces of obvious Middle Eastern derivation appeared in the hands of non-noble French cavalry and infantry in the 13th century; while the late 13th–14th century *goedendag*, primarily a Flemish infantry weapon, had a spiked head set in a massive wooden

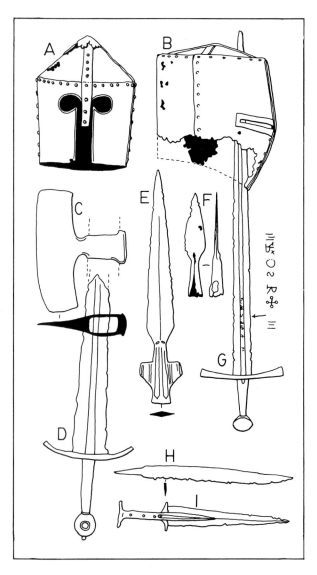

(A) Helmet said to date from 13th or 14th century, perhaps a fake (Mus. de l'Armée, Paris). (B) Late 13th century great helm (Mus. d'Art, Paris). (C) 11th century axe from Colletière, probably a work tool rather than a weapon. (D) Mid-14th century sword with reliquary set into the pommel (Mus. de l'Armée, *Paris). (E) 11th century spear from Colletière. (F) 11th century javelin from Colletière. (G) Sword c.1150–75, with inlaid decoration on the blade (private coll., Paris). (H) 11th century dagger or knife from Colletière. (I) Early one-piece form of Burgundian basilard dagger (Boissonas Coll., Geneva).*

shaft, perhaps designed to injure horses as much as their riders. It was clearly very cheap and was available to anyone; those made in Gent in 1304 cost only one-tenth of a shield, which was itself among the cheapest items of equipment.

Among missile weapons, various forms of javelin such as the *agier* were still recorded in the late 11th century, while the simple hand bow was never abandoned. Of far greater importance was the crossbow. This had survived as a hunting weapon in many corners of Western Europe, particularly around the Mediterranean, after the fall of the Roman Empire. Crossbows may have been used in defence of Senlis in AD 947, and there were almost certainly crossbowmen with William the Conqueror's Army at Hastings in 1066. Mounted crossbowmen formed a highly mobile élite in various early 13th century French armies, and by the early 14th century they were as important in open warfare as they had long been in sieges. Other bulkier siege engines could also be used in the open against a static foe, as the French did against immobile Flemish infantry at the battle of Mons-en-Pevèle in 1304. The terrifying *espringal*, which shot a massive bolt or arrow, was also used by the French aboard Meuse river-craft that same year.

Further reading

E. Audouin, *Essai sur L'Armée Royale au Temps de Philippe Auguste* (1913).

T. N. Bisson, *Medieval France and her Pyrenean Neighbours* (1989).

M. Bloch (trans. L. A. Manyon), *Feudal Society* (1961).

P. Contamine (trans. M. Jones), *War in the Middle Ages* (1984).

G. Duby, *Hommes et Structures du Moyen Âge: Recueil d'articles* (1973).

Funck-Brentano, *Féodalité et Chevalerie* (1946).

La Guerre et la Paix, Frontières et Violences au Moyen Âge (Actes du 101e Congrès National des Sociétés Savants: Lille 1976) (1978)

E. M. Hallam, Capetian France 987–1328 (1980).

C. Harper-Bill & R. Harvey (edits), The Ideals and Practice of Medieval Knighthood (Papers from the first and second Strawberry Hill Conferences) (1986).

A. R. Lewis, 'Le féodalité dans le Toulousain et la France méridionale (850–1050)', Annales du Midi LXXVI/2 (1964).

A. Luchaire, Les Communes Françaises à l'époque des Capétiens Directs (1980).

W. M. Newman, Le Domaine Royal sous les Premiers Capétiens (987–1180) (1937).

S. Painter, French Chivalry: Chivalric Ideas and Practices in Medieval France (1940).

D. J. A. Ross, 'L'Originalité de Turoldus: le maniement de la lance', Cahiers de Civilizations Médiévale VI (1963).

J. R. Strayer, The Reign of Philip the Fair (1980).

J. F. Verbruggen, The Art of Warfare in Western Europe during the Middle Ages (1977).

The Château de Val, a typical early 14th century French castle built in 1322 in the Auvergne region. A church is incorporated into the outer defence. (Author's photograph)

THE PLATES

A: The 11th century:
A1: Northern French miles warrior
There was a lot of uniformity in the arms of Western European cavalry in the 11th century. This man has an early form of mail *hauberk* slit at the sides. The *ventail* to protect his face is shown unlaced, while his sword is thrust through a slit in the *hauberk* into a scabbard and belt worn beneath. His shield is of the large so-called 'Norman' type. (Main sources: spear from Colletière, Dauphiné; 'Fortitude', statue late 11th cent. Cluny Mus., Paris)

A2: Southern French miles
This warrior has a one-piece helmet on which the metal strips are merely decorative, but lacks body armour. Note the early form of 'heraldic' design on his shield, and his horse's early but complicated curb bit. (Main sources: carved capitals, late 11th cent. *in situ* church of Ste. Foy, Conques, cloisters of Abbey of St. Pierre, Moissac, & church of St. Nectaire;

Atlantic Bible, south French 11th cent. Ms. Edili 126, Bib. Laur. Florence)

A3: Southern French peasant levy
Here a southern peasant watches his son span an early form of hunting crossbow in a way shown in the earliest illustrations. He is also armed with a massive war-axe. (Main sources: crossbow from Colletière, Dauphiné, 11th cent.; carved capital, c.1096, *in situ* Cathedral, Toulouse)

B: First half 12th century:
B1: King Louis VI The Fat
In the first half of the 12th century arms and armour differed only in detail from those seen earlier. The sleeves of mail *hauberks* grew longer, while a forward-curved one-piece helmet became widespread; its shape probably indicated that the front was thicker than the sides and rear. War-saddles were now of the fully developed peaked type. (Main sources: sword, French mid-12th cent. private coll. Ely; enamelled tomb slab of Geoffrey of Anjou, early 12th cent. Archaeol. Mus. Le Mans; carved tympanum, c.1125, *in situ* Cathedral, Angoulême)

B2: Seigneur of a castle
The main features distinguishing this knight are his large rectangular shield for infantry combat, a simpler helmet with a large nasal fastened to its brow-

band, and the sword-belt being worn outside his *hauberk*. The device on his shield is that traditionally given to the lords of Chalo. (Main sources: painted chest, mid-12th cent. Cathedral Treasury, Vannes; carved tympanum 1120–30, *in situ* Church of Ste. Foy, Conques; enamelled box from Limoges, French 1150–1200, Brit. Mus., London)

B3: French militiaman, early 12th century

This man has very simple equipment, except for his framed iron helmet. He has a knife and buckler shield for close combat but carries a substantial staff–sling, perhaps to hurl rocks at the defenders of a castle. (Main sources: carved capitals, late 11th–early 12th cents. *in situ* church, St. Nectaire; ivory chess piece, southern French 12th cent. Bargello Mus. Florence)

C: Second half 12th century:
C1: Spanish mercenary knight in service of English Gascony, c.1187–88

This knight has an extraordinary helmet seen for a few years in Castile and Cantabria. It appears to be made of an ordinary forward-tilted helmet, plus a rigid visor and an additional neck protection at the back. (Main sources: carved capitals & reliefs, mid–late 12th cent. *in situ* church at Rebolledo della Torre, Santa Maria la Real at Sanguessa & Cathedral cloisters, Tudela; *Bible of King Sancho of Navarre*, 1197, Ms. 108, Bib. Munic. Amiens)

C2: Southern French infantryman

This man has a new form of low-domed helmet without a nasal; his long-bladed weapon is shown in

'Warriors on top of an allegorical tower', Speculum Theologiae, French early 14th century. The central figure has a normal chapel-de-fer helmet. Those next to him have plain mail coifs and the outer warriors appear to wear helmets with brims or peaks only at the front. The man on the left also has a massive hinged bevor to protect his neck. (Ms. Ars. 1037, f.3, Bib. Nat., Paris)

various illustrations and may be the *faussart* of the written sources. (Main sources: carved friezes, mid–12th cent. *in situ* west front of church, St. Giles du Gard; 'Goliath', in *La Charité Psalter*, French late 12th cent. Ms. Harl. 2895, Brit. Lib.; 'Flight into Egypt', carved capital, 1120–30, *in situ* Cathedral, Autun; *Reliquary of St. Hadelin*, 1150–75, Treasury of Church of St. Martin, Visé)

C3: Navarrese mercenary infantryman

This man's costume betrays the Islamic influence felt even in the far north of Spain, as does the construction of his leather shield. His *dard* javelin was the characteristic weapon of the Pyrenean mountaineers. (Main sources: dagger from upper city of Vitoria, 12th cent. Alava Regional Mus. Vitoria; *Bible of King Sancho of Navarre*, 1197, Ms. 108, Bib. Munic. Amiens)

D: The army of Philip Augustus, early 13th century:
D1: The Sire de Montfort, c.1215

The young lord De Montfort has been given the most up-to-date knightly arms and armour, including a padded *coif* worn inside his mail *coif* and designed to support a helmet with a fixed face-mask. His mail

hauberk also includes mittens, and is worn beneath a partially padded surcoat, while his legs are fully protected by mail *chausses*. The *caparison* of De Montfort's *destrier* includes a protective quilted head piece. (Main sources: wall paintings, late 12th–early 13th cent. *in situ* Templar Church, Cressac; stained-glass windows, late 12th–early 13th cents. *in situ* Cathedral, Chartres)

D2: Brabançon knight being armed, c.1225

Here we can see the quilted *gambeson* worn beneath a mail *hauberk* and the linen *coif* which includes a padded ring to support an early type of 'great helm'; over his knees the knight also wears quilted *cuisses*. (Main sources: lost funerary slab of Nicola III de Rumigny, late 12th–early 13th cent. after Van Dun Berg & Roland; aquamanile in form of a knight, French or German 1200–50, Bargello Mus. Florence; *Chest of Abbé Nantelme*, 1225, Treasury, Abbey of St. Maurice, Switzerland)

D3: French squire

The only military equipment worn by this non-combatant squire would be a close-fitting iron *cervellière* helmet and a dagger in a tooled leather sheath tied to his belt. (Main sources: *Maciejowski Bible*, French c.1250, Pierpont Morgan Lib. New York;

Roman de Toute Chevalerie, French 13th cent. Ms. Fr. 23464, Bib. Nat. Paris)

E: The last Albigensian rising, mid-13th century:

E1: Southern French sergeant from County of Foix

This soldier wears an iron helmet with a strengthening ridge down the centre. Scale cuirasses appear in various 13th century French sources and one such armour survives in neighbouring Spain. Otherwise he has an old-fashioned kite-shaped shield now only used by foot soldiers. (Main sources: *Maciejowski Bible*, French c.1250, Pierpont Morgan Lib. New York; carved reliefs & capitals, early 13th cent. *in situ* Church of St. Trophime, Arles)

E2: French royal knight

In hot climates Western knights often wore the *chapel-de-fer* helmets normally associated with *sergeants*. This man's shield is now much smaller, while a buckled sword-belt has replaced the knotted type. On his right shoulder is a single thin wooden *ailette* showing the arms adopted by the Curés de Neuilly-sur-Marne after the Fourth Crusade. (Main sources: tomb slab of Georges de Niverlée, c.1262, *in situ* church, Niverlée; *Album of Villard de Honnecourt*,

French mid-13th cent. Ms. Fr. 19.093, Bib. Nat. Paris)

E3: Southern French crossbowman from Bigorre

Quilted soft-armours were often worn by infantry-men without mail *hauberks*. This crossbowman, with his typical 13th century 'stirrup' crossbow, and doubled spanning hook hung from his belt, also has an early form of *basilard* dagger. (Main sources: *Maciejowski Bible*, French c.1250, Pierpont Morgan Lib. New York; relief carvings, 13th cent. *in situ* west front of Cathedral, Amiens)

F: The French invasion of Aragon, late 13th century:

F1: French infantry sergeant from Toulouse

Fully armoured foot soldiers probably remained a minority, but this man has a full mail *hauberk* over a padded *gambeson* apparently fastened to the neck of

Laane castle, first erected in the 12th century as an outer protection for the city of Gent but extensively rebuilt in the 17th century. Like most fortifications in the low-lying west of Flanders, Laane has a water-filled moat. (Author's photograph)

the *hauberk* which may, however, have been a separate *collière*. Also note the close-fitting *cervelière* helmet, the rigid knee *poleyns* attached to the leather *cuisses*, and the long-bladed *guisarme* axe. (Main sources: 'The Betrayal' statue group, north French 1275–1300, Met. Mus. New York; *Chasse de Sainte-Gertrude*, c.1272, Treasury of Church of St. Gertrude, Nivelles; *Romance of Lancelot*, south French late 13th cent. Deulofeu Coll. Puigcerda)

F2: French military engineer

The helmet worn by this man is of one-piece construction with a very narrow brim. Yet it might still be called a *chapel-de-fer*. In addition he has a *hauberk* beneath his *supertunic* and carries a fine Spanish sword. (Main sources: effigy of Jean

45

d'Alluye, French mid-13th cent. Cloisters Mus. New York; *Apocalypse of St. John*, French late 13th cent. Brit. Lib.)

F3: Aragonese light cavalryman of Cardona family

The light cavalry of Catalonia and Aragon would evolve into the light horsemen *à la jineta* characteristic of later medieval Spain. Many had full mail *hauberks*, light helmets and large round shields, but this man also seems to have a thickly padded armour beneath his surcoat. The peculiar object behind the saddle, shown on an Aragonese carving, is here interpreted as a seat for an infantryman. (Main sources: relief carving from Poblet Monastery, late 13th cent. Met. Mus. New York)

G: Battle of Courtrai, 1302:
G1: French knight

In the 14th century 'great helms' would be relegated to the tournament, but this knight still wears a simple version built up of riveted sections. Beneath his *hauberk* is a fabric-covered coat-of-plates, while his mail *chausses* show the outline of rigid greaves

beneath. Large domed *poleyns* protect his knees. The man wields a heavy *falchion*; and his horse is protected by a full mail bard with a quilted lining. (Main sources: *History of William of Tyre*, French early 14th cent. Ms. Fr. 352, Bib. Nat. Paris; *Les Chroniques de St. Denis*, French early 14th cent. Ms. Roy. 16.G.VI, Brit. Lib. London; *Histoire du Bon Roi Alexandre*, French c.1300, Ms. 11040, Bib. Royale, Brussels)

G2: Senior Flemish militiaman

The metal-lined coat-of-plates worn by this man was seen in both France and Germany. The rest of his equipment includes a *chapel-de-fer* worn over a close-fitting *cervellière* and gauntlets covered with whalebone scales. The spiked *goedendag* 'mace' was closely associated with Flemish infantry. (Main sources: *Courtrai Chest*, Flemish early 14th cent. New College, Oxford; 'Massacre of the Innocents', German late 13th cent. Ms. Add. 17,687, Brit. Lib.; 'Massacre of the Innocents', relief carvings 13th cent. *in situ* church, Norrey; brass tomb-slab of Sir Brocardus de Charpignie, French late 13th cent. location unknown)

'Flemish militia at the battle of Courtrai', The Courtrai Chest, *Flemish early 14th century. Now proved to date from shortly after the battle of Courtrai, this carved chest celebrates militia victories over French Royal armies during the early 14th century Flemish uprising. Here crossbowmen shoot behind a row of long spears while men armed with heavy spiked* goedendags *stand behind them. (New College Library, Oxford; author's photograph)*

Légende de St. Denis, French c.1317. Although the seated man on the left wears fanciful scale armour, the rest of the equipment appears to be genuine, including scale-covered gauntlets. Note the quilted neck and leg defences of the man with the curved falchion and the small round buckler hung on the scabbard of a man on the far right. (Ms. Fr. 2090–2, f.129r, Paris)

G3: Flemish urban militia crossbowman

Most militiamen would have simpler equipment like this man, who is protected by a close-fitting *cervellière* and a basic mail *hauberk*. His buckler shield has a reinforced iron rim. His crossbow was spanned by a new system of hooks and pulleys, also hanging from his belt. (Main sources: shield from Amsterdam, 13th–14th cent.; sword, mid-13th cent. Landesmuseum, Zurich; *The Courtrai Chest*, Flemish early 14th cent. New College, Oxford; *Shrine of St. Odilia*, painted chest 1292, Treasury of Monastery of Kolen-Sittard-Kerniel)

Knightly dubbing ceremony, c.1328: French baron

Here a senior lord wears a complicated *chaperon* hat and a wide-sleeved *garnache* cloak over his tunic. (Main sources: carvings of 1324 *in situ* Westminster Abbey, London)

H2: French squire being dubbed

The costume of younger men differed from that of their elders primarily in a preference for shorter tunics. This man also carries a thicker-bladed sword designed to penetrate armour, while his scabbard is attached to the sword-belt in a simpler manner which may have entered France from Catalonia. (Main sources: French sword, 1300–50, Archaeol. Mus. Madrid; unnamed effigy, early 14th cent. *in situ* Poblet Monastery, Tarragona)

H3: French knight

Here a knight has an early form of *bascinet* helmet and a massive *bevor* to cover his neck and shoulders, plus iron gauntlets and iron leg armour. His large sword is a cavalry sword-of-war, and he is also armed with a substantial dagger. (Main sources: effigy of Thibaud de Pomollain, c.1330, *in situ* church, Coulommiers; 'Galahad', carved ivory box, French early 14th cent. Met. Mus. New York)

47

Notes sur les planches en couleur

A1 Une des premières sortes de haubert à mailles, fendu sur les côtés. Le ventail de protection du visage n'est pas lacé ici. L'épée est passée dans une fente ménagée dans le haubert, qui ouvre sur un fourreau porté sous le haubert. Bouclier de type "normand". **A2** Un casque en une pièce avec rayures décoratives. Le bouclier porte un motif "héraldique" ancien. Le personnage n'a pas d'armure pour le corps. Le cheval porte un mors de type ancien mais compliqué. **A3** Un paysan du sud regarde son fils bander une ancienne arbalète de chasse. Le paysan est aussi armé d'une hache de guerre.

B1 Haubert à mailles à manches longues, un casque fait d'une pièce courbé en avant. Une selle complète de guerre avec pointe. **B2** Grand bouclier rectangulair pour combat d'infanterie, un casque plus simple avec un grand nasal plutôt attaché au frontal. La ceinture d'épée se porte au dehors du haubert. L'emblème sur le bouclier est celui des seigneurs de Chalo. **B3** Equipement simple mis à part le casque à structure de fer. Il porte un couteau, un bouclier et une bandoulière à bâton.

C1 Un casque ordinaire incliné en avant avec un viseur rigide et une protection pour le cou. Cette conception fut utilisée pendant quelques années en Castille et à Cantabria. **C2** Casque à dôme bas sans nasal. L'arme à longue lame pourrait être le faussart. **C3** Les vêtements et le bouclier de cuir trahit l'influence islamique. Le javelot dard était l'arme caractéristique des montagnards pyrénéens.

D1 Le jeune De Montfort porte l'armure la plus moderne. Une coif matelassée se trouve à l'intérieur de sa coif de maille. La coif est conçue pour soutenir un casque avec un masque fixe pour le visage. Le haubert de mailles comprend des mitaines et se porte au dessous d'un surcot en partie matelassé. Les jambes sont protégées par des chausses de mailles. Le caparison comprend une pièce protectrice rembourrée pour la tête. **D2** Un gambison matelassé, porté en général au dessous du haubert de mailles, et une coif de toile, comprenant une bague rembourrée pour soutenir un ancien "grand casque". Il porte des cuissardes matelassées au dessous de genoux. **D3** Le seul équipement que porte ce propriétaire terrien non-combattant est un casque cervelière en fer bien ajusté et une dague.

E1 Casque de fer avec crête de consolidation au milieu, cuirasse en écailles, et bouclier à l'ancienne mode en forme de losange. **E2** Casque Chapel-de-fer, un bouclier de conception plus petite et une ceinture d'épée à boucle plutôt qu'à noeud. Sur son épaule droite, une simple ailette de bois porte les armes des Curés de Neuilly-sur-Marne. **E3** Armure souple matelassée portée sans haubert à mailles, une arbalète à étrivières caractéristique du XIIIe siècle, et un double crochet ouvert attaché à la ceinture. Il a une ancienne forme de dague basilard.

F1 Haubert complet à mailles au dessus d'un gambison matelassé, un casque cervelière bien ajusté, poleyns rigides pour les genoux, attachés à des cuissardes de cuir, et une hache guisarme à longue lame. **F2** Un chapel-de-fer de bonne qualité et un haubert sous sa tunique de dessus. Il porte également une fine épée espagnole. **F3** Haubert complet de mailles, casque léger et grand bouclier. Il a aussi une armure à rembourrage épais en dessous de son surcot. L'objet curieux qui se trouve derrière la selle pourrait être un siège pour un fantassin.

G1 Un simple "grand casque" fait de sections rivetées. En dessous de son haubert se trouve une cotte de mailles recouverte de toile, alors que ses chausses de mailles laissent voir le contour de cretons rigides au dessous. De larges poleyns en forme de dôme protègent ses genoux et il manie un lourd falchion. Le cheval est protégé par une barde toute de mailles avec une doublure matelassée. **G2** Une cotte de mailles doublée de métal, un chapel-de-fer porté au-dessus d'une cervelière ajustée, des gantelets couverts d'écailles de baleine et une masse d'arme à pointes goedendag. **G3** Une cervelière, un haubert de mailles simples et un bouclier avec un rebord métallique renforcé. Son arbalète était tendue par un système de crochets et de poulies accroché à la ceinture.

H1 Le grand seigneur porte un chaperon compliqué et un manteau garnacle à manches larges sur sa tunique. **H2** Les hommes plus jeunes préféraient une tunique plus courte et une épée à lame plus épaisse conçue pour pénétrer les armures. Son fourreau est attaché à la ceinture selon une mode qui aurait pu venir de Catalogne. **H3** Un des premiers modèles de casque bascinet et un bevor massif qui couvre le cou et les épaules. Il a aussi des gantelets de fer et une protection de jambe, un grand sabre-de-guerre de la cavalerie et une dague de dimension substantielle.

Farbtafeln

A1 Eine frühe Form von Panzerhemd, an den Seiten geschlitzt. Der Ventail-Gesichtsschutz ist hier geöffnet gezeigt. Das Schwert wird durch einen Schlitz im Panzerhemd in eine darunter getragene Scheide gesteckt. Schild nach Normannen-Art. **A2** Ein einteiliger Helm mit Verzierungsstreifen. Der Schild zeigt ein frühes Wappenzeichen. Die Figur trägt keine Rüstung. Das Pferd zeigt ein frühes, aber komplexes Zaumzeug. **A3** Ein südlicher Bauer sieht seinem Sohn zu, wie er versucht, eine frühe-Jagd-Armbrust zu spannen. Der Bauer ist auch mit einer Streitaxt bewaffnet.

B1 Panzerhemd mit langen Ärmeln, ein nach vorne gekrümmter, einteiliger Helm. Ein vollentwickelter Kampfsattel. **B2** Großer rechteckiger Schild für Infanteriekampf, ein einfacher Helm mit großem Nasenschutz, angebracht am Stirnband. Der Schwertgurt wird über dem Panzerhemds getragen. Das Zeichen auf dem Schild ist das der Herren von Chalo. **B3** Einfache Ausrüstung, abgesehen von dem Eisenhelm. Er trägt ein messer, einen kleinen Rundschild und eine Steinschleuder.

C1 Ein gewöhnlicher, nach vorne geneigter Helm mit festem Visier und Nacken = schutz. Diese Form war einige Jahre lang in Kastilien und Kantabrien üblich. **C2** Helm mit niedrigem Kopf und ohne Nasenschutz. Die Waffe mit ihrer langen Klinge könnte ein Faussart sein. **C3** Kleidung und Lederschild zeigen islamischen Einfluß. Der Dard-Speer war die typische Waffe pyrenäischer Gebirgsbewohner.

D1 Der junge De Montfort trägt die neueste Rüstung. Eine gepolsterte Coif innerhalb der Panzer-Coifs. Die Coif oder Helmkappe ist dafür konstruiert, einen helm mit festem Visier zu tragen. Zum Panzerhemd gehören Fausthandschuhe, und über dem Hemd wird ein teilweise gepolsterter Überwurf getragen. Die Beine werden von Panzer-Chausses geschützt. Die Caparison oder Schabracke hat auch ein gestepptes Kopf-Schutzstück. **D2** Ein gestepptes, gefüttertes Wams, normalerweise unter dem Panzerhemd getragen, und eine Leinen-Helmkappe mit einem gepolsterten Ring zur Stütze eines großen, frühen Helms. Er trägt wattierte Knieschützer. **D3** Die einzige Ausrüstung dieses nicht kämpfenden Gutsherrn ist ein eng anliegender Cervelliere-Helm und ein Dolch.

E1 Eisenhelm mit Verstärkungswulst im Zentrum, Schuppenküraß, altomidscher Schild. **E2** Chapel-de-fer-Helm, kleinerer Schild, Schwertgurt, nicht verknotet. Auf seiner rechten Schulter eine hölzerne Ailette mit dem Wappen der Curés de Neuilly-sur-Marne. **E3** Wattierte Rüstung ohne Panzerhemd, eine typische Armbrust des 13. Jahrhunderts, mit Doppelspannhaken am Gürtel. Frühe Form eines Basilard-Dolchs.

F1 Komplettes Panzerhemd über einem gepolsterten (Gambeson (Wams), eng anliegender Cervelliere-Helm, starre Poleyns-Knieschützer, verbunden mit Leder-Cuisses, und eine Guisarme-Axt. **F2** Chapel-de-fer bester Qualität und ein Panzerhemd unter seinem Überwurf. Er trägt auch ein erstklassiges spanisches Schwert. **F3** Komplettes Panzerhemd, leichter Helm und großer Schild. Unter seinem Überwurf trägt er eine dick gepolsterte Rüstung. Das seltsame Objekt hinter dem Sattel dürfte ein Hilfssitz für einen Infanteristen sein.

G1 Ein einfacher großer Helm aus Einzelteilen zusammengenietet. Unter dem Panzerhemd befindet sich ein stoffbespanntes Coat-of-plates, während seine Chausses die Umrisse der darunterliegenden, starren Beinschienen erkennen lassen. Große, gewölbte Poleyns schützen seine Knie, und er schwingt einen schweren Falchion (Krummsäbel). Das Pferd ist durch ein komplettes Panzerband mit gestepptem Futter geschützt. **G2** Ein metallgefüttertes Coat-of-plates, ein Chapel-de-fer über einem eng anliegenden Cervelliere-Helm, Walbei-Schuppen und ein Goedendag-Morgenstern. **G3** Ein Cervelliere, ein einfaches Panzerhemd und ein kleiner Rundschild mit eisenverstärktem Rand. Seine Armbrust wurde durch ein System von Haken und Rädern gespannt, die vo[ ] seinem Gürtel hängen.

H1 Dieser Aristokrat trägt einen komplizierten Chaperon-Hut und einen Garnac[ ] Umhang mit weiten Ärmeln über seiner Bluse. **H2** Eine kürzere Bluse, bevorz[ ] von jüngeren Männern, und ein Schwert mit starrkerer Klinge, um eine Rüst[ ] durchdringen zu können. Die Scheide ist an seinem Gürtel auf eine Weise befes[ ] die aus katalonien stammt. **H3** Ein früher Bascinet-Helm mit massivem Bevor[ ] Nacken und Schultern. Er hat auch Eisenhandschuhe und Beinschienen, ein g[ ] Kavallerieschwert und einen großen Dolch.